*A First World War AEC Y-type, modernised in 1930 and fitted with a five-cylinder Gardner 5L2 diesel. An LW (lightweight) range of three-, four-, five- and six-cylinder diesels specially for vehicles followed in 1931.*

# Proprietary Engines for Vehicles

## Nick Baldwin

# A Shire book
*in association with the Michael Sedgwick Trust*

# Contents

This work is published with the assistance of the Michael Sedgwick Trust. Founded in memory of the famous motoring researcher and author Michael Sedgwick (1926–83), the Trust is a Registered Charity to encourage the publishing of new research and recording of motoring history. Suggestions for future projects or donations should be sent to the Hon. Sec. of the Michael Sedgwick Trust, c/o the National Motor Museum, Beaulieu, Hampshire SO42 7ZN, England.

Cover: *A White & Poppe four-cylinder pair-cast engine with fixed cylinder heads and transverse drive to magneto and water pump; from an early sales catalogue.*

British Library Cataloguing in Publication Data: Baldwin, Nick. Proprietary engines for vehicles. – (A Shire album; 360) 1. Automobiles – Motors I. Title 629.2'504. ISBN 0 7478 0496 6.

Editorial Consultant: Michael E. Ware, former Director of the National Motor Museum, Beaulieu.

*Published in 2001 by Shire Publications Ltd, Cromwell House, Church Street, Princes Risborough, Buckinghamshire HP27 9AA, UK. (Website: www.shirebooks.co.uk)*
*Copyright © 2001 by Nick Baldwin. First published 2001. Shire Album 360. ISBN 0 7478 0496 6.*
*Nick Baldwin is hereby identified as the author of this work in accordance with Section 77 of the Copyright, Designs and Patents Act 1988.*

Printed in Great Britain by CIT Printing Services Ltd, Press Buildings, Merlins Bridge, Haverfordwest, Pembrokeshire SA61 1XF.

# The pioneer years

In the years from 1900 to 1930 most vehicle-makers made neither their own bodywork nor their own engines. They were chassis-manufacturers and they left these other tasks to outside firms.

The great pioneers Gottlieb Daimler and Carl Benz produced their first vehicles in 1885–6 and soon licensed other car-makers to use similar engines. Daimler in Coventry and Panhard & Levassor in Paris entered the motor business via Gottlieb Daimler. Panhard also supplied Peugeot and a dozen others with engines. Benz engines were used by Roger and Hurtu in France, Marshall, Arnold and Star in Britain, and Mueller in the USA. The Benz engine firm ultimately became a separate entity, MWM – the initials of the Motor Werke Mannheim, and MWM engines are specified, notably in farm tractors, to this day.

Wilhelm Maybach, who had helped Gottlieb Daimler with his early designs, left to set up his own business in 1907. Maybach proprietary engines were found in many types of machine, notably Zeppelin dirigibles in the early years and Dutch Spyker 30/40 hp six-cylinder luxury cars in 1920.

Another famous early name was N. A. Otto, the inventor of the four-stroke cycle. His engines were made by Deutz, and Crossley Brothers became British patent holders in 1867. Crossley went on to become a major engine-maker, mostly for industrial purposes, but also built vehicles from 1904.

Count de Dion and his mechanic Georges Bouton had meanwhile revolutionised small engines by inventing in 1895 a coil ignition system that allowed many more revolutions per minute than other engines. Their original 137 cc motor was capable of 2000 rpm whereas a typical hot bulb or trembler coil engine could rarely exceed 1000 rpm. Higher rpm produced more power in relation to cylinder capacity and soon de Dion-Bouton was selling far more engines than motorcycles, tricycles and light cars. In the years up to 1914 approximately 160 car-makers around the world employed de Dion-Bouton engines: seventy-one were French, including Corré, Clément, Delage and Hurtu; forty-seven were British,

*Georges Bouton in December 1894 astride the first de Dion-Bouton tricycle powered by his high-speed, air-cooled engine with trembler coil ignition.*

3

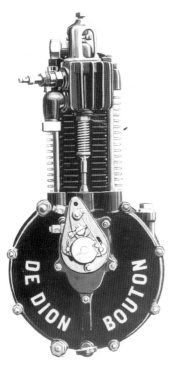

*The de Dion-Bouton engine, like many early rivals, had atmospheric inlet and mechanical exhaust valves. Battery ignition enabled it to attain an unprecedented 2000 rpm.*

including Argyll, Alldays, Dennis, Humber and Star; and ten each were Belgian and German.

Hundreds of car-makers appeared in the years leading up to the First World War, very few of whom could afford to develop their own engines. As a result a separate engine-manufacturing industry grew up, particularly in Britain, France and the USA.

Some of the firms that became involved in the industry were already established in other types of business. In Britain sanitary engineers Tylor had just a few car customers but several commercial-vehicle users, notably Karrier and London bus builder AEC.

Sidney Dawson Begbie organised a British outlet for French Aster engines in 1899 and then opened a factory at Wembley in 1900. The two factories soon catered for over 130 vehicle builders around the world. By 1912 Aster claimed to have built 18,500 engines, though not all had been for vehicles. Whilst the French factory outlived the Second World War the British one went into voluntary liquidation in 1927 and was merged with Scottish car-maker Arrol Johnston, only to vanish in the 1930s, when its London premises became Singer Motors' service department. Aster's last few engines in the 1930s were actually built for it by Meadows.

In Coventry Alfred White, the son of a director of the Swift bicycle firm, met his

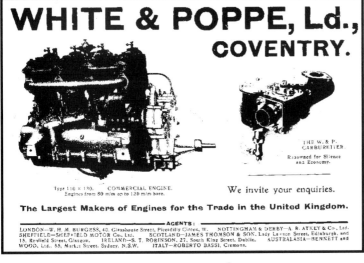

# WHITE & POPPE, Ld.,
## COVENTRY.

Type 110 × 130.   COMMERCIAL ENGINE.
Engines from 80 m/m up to 120 m/m bore.

THE W. & P. CARBURETER.
Renowned for Silence and Economy.

We invite your enquiries.

**The Largest Makers of Engines for the Trade in the United Kingdom.**

*A 1908 White & Poppe advertisement. Four separately cast cylinders with non-detachable cylinder heads were typical, though Ford had just pioneered monobloc fours with removable heads, which would become universal.*

4

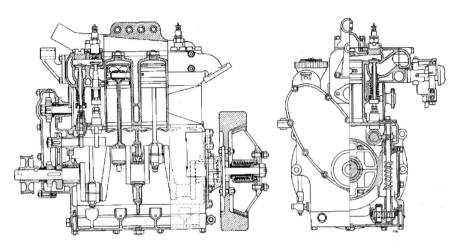

*A contemporary of White & Poppe in Coventry was Johnson, Hurley & Martin. This is a sectional drawing of its Alpha 11 hp monobloc 1330 cc four-cylinder motor in 1915. Approximately twenty car firms became Alpha customers.*

Norwegian partner Peter Poppe on a visit to the Steyr factory in Austria. They formed White & Poppe in 1899 to make fuses, carburettors and engines. Swift was one of the first important customers; by 1906 there were fourteen more. In 1909 White & Poppe made 576 engines and in 1911 the figure was 982. In 1919 the firm was bought by Dennis, which had long used its engines, its factory later becoming home to Triumph. Members of the Poppe family reached senior positions at Dennis and Rover in the 1920s.

White & Poppe's most famous legacy is, however, its involvement with the Morris

*The 11 hp Alpha had a side-valve L-head (earlier types had T-heads with separate camshafts operating inlet and exhaust valves). Ignition was by magneto and there was pressure lubrication. The four holes in the water-pipe castings carried the high-tension plug leads.*

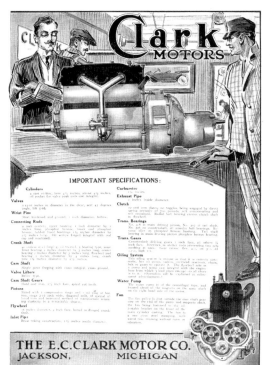

THE COLUMBIA POWER UNIT.

Above: *The Columbia of 1915 came in 2.3 and 3 litre sizes, which would have made them a little too large to be popular when horsepower taxation was introduced in Britain in 1921. The box on the side was an early example of an electric starter, which also doubled as a dynamo.*

Left: *Clark was one of dozens of US rivals in 1912. The monobloc layout with in-unit gearbox and water pump as opposed to thermo syphon cooling was advanced, but the splash lubrication was not.*

Oxford, a successful British attempt to mass-produce an assembled car in 1913. That year 393 cars were made, followed by 907 in 1914. White & Poppe soon found that it could not compete on price terms with Continental, a US manufacturer, which quoted £18 against nearly £50 for the British engine. After 1133 Continental-powered Morris Oxfords had been sold in the war years Morris managed to arrange for a copy to be

*A 1913 advertisement for British Aster showing single-, twin- and six-cylinder engines. The six-cylinder unit, with three blocks of two cylinders, could be specified in Merryweather fire appliances.*

*The Milwaukee area was home to, amongst others, Le Roi, Johnson, Milwaukee Motors and Wisconsin. This advertisement describes the advanced features for 1909 of pressure lubrication and dual ignition (but note the misprint of 'send'!).*

# The Different and Better Motor

Wisconsin Motors are different because they are better:
—and better because they are different. In designing them,
we built on the merits of many other motors—added distinctive features to overcome the weaknesses of every other
make:—and have produced a distinctive type of Gasoline
motor, keeping every good old feature and none of the bad ones.

| How it is Different | Why it is Better |
| --- | --- |
| Has crank shaft of large diameter......Added strength. | |
| Double ignition system............ | Using either magneto or battery, or both. |
| Self-contained oiling system sup-plied by gear pump through hollow crank-shaft ...................... | Least possible danger and nuisance from poor oiling. |
| Larger bearings than any other mo-tor .................................... | Increased length of life. |
| Has very large valves...............Develops more power. | |

**4 Cylinder—4 Cycle     40-45 H. P.     4 3-4" Bore—5 1-2" Stroke**

And these differences—these virtues of materials, mechanical construc-
tion and skilled work—produce a motor that is as far in front of
ordinary motors as ordinary motors are ahead of hand power.

## To Manufacturers of Automobiles

We are in a position to fill quantity orders; we
want them to prove to you our claim that the
Wisconsin Motor will add greatly to the
value of any car on the market, because
of its distinctive features and its
unquestioned superiority over
every motor on the market.
*Write for our
proposition to-day.*

WISCONSIN MOTOR
MFG. CO., N. Mil-
waukee, Wis.
Dept. 26

*SIGN AND TEAR OFF THIS COUPON AND SEND US AT ONCE*

Wisconsin
Motor Mfg. Co.,
North Milwaukee,
Wis.

Gentlemen:

Without cost or obligation you may
send your proposition to us—at once.

Name .................................

Address .................................

*The series-production V eight was pioneered by de Dion-Bouton in 1909. They were used in its own cars though its proprietary-engine customers tended to buy far smaller units. As on many contemporary types of engine, the visible caps were for extricating the valves through non-detachable heads, whilst the taps reduced compression for hand-starting and could act as petrol primers.*

7

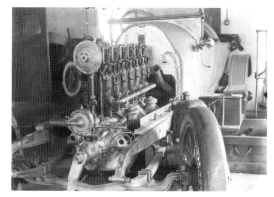

*Hall-Scott made 13.5 litre overhead camshaft engines for the 125 bhp Fageol, the USA's most powerful car of 1917. After powering Fageol and ACF buses, the firm made heavy-vehicle engines to the early 1960s, latterly affiliated to Hercules.*

built in the Hotchkiss armaments factory in Coventry, soon acquired by Morris.

Hotchkiss's origins had been in making guns in the USA and then in Paris but it added motor components to its product list and, from 1903, complete cars in France. At least eight car and five commercial-vehicle firms came to use Hotchkiss engines.

Continental had started in 1902 as the Autocar Equipment Company but had soon changed its name to Continental in honour of a trip taken by its designers to Europe to study the latest developments. It employed six hundred men in 1906 and ten years later claimed to be the largest manufacturer of motors alone in the world.

H. M. Leland made engines for the original Olds and for Cadillac, the world's best-selling cars of 1905. David Buick also entered the industry with proprietary engines for the infant Detroit industry before creating the car firm bearing his name in 1903.

Edward Ballot had made marine engines in Paris from 1906 and his anchor emblem was soon found on engines supplied to almost fifty road-vehicle makers. Ballot made Hispano-Suiza aero engines during the First World War and their technology was used on high-performance car engines tried on a series of Ballot racing cars. Ballot soon became better known for sporting cars for road use than proprietary engines and was absorbed by Hispano-Suiza in 1930.

Amongst other French engine-makers were Altos (with fourteen vehicle customers), Fivet (nine, including AC in Britain in 1913 before it tried Anzani), Mutel (eighteen), Sergant (eight) and Ydral (nine). Fivet had grown from the 1902 Tony Huber car business that was refinanced in 1905 by a group of businessmen including Armand Peugeot to make proprietary engines.

*Rutenber of Marion, Indiana, made this tribloc six as well as monobloc fours in 1912. Albert C. Barley controlled car-makers Halladay and Roamer as well as Rutenber, which was a successor to the Western Motor Company founded in 1902 or possibly earlier.*

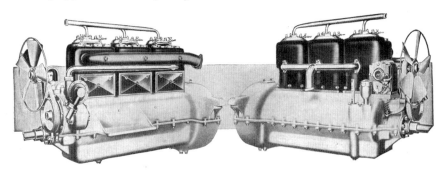

# The 1920s unfold

There were 109,705 cars on the roads of Britain in 1919 and 1,075,081 in 1930. Mass-production had arrived and, in general, successful firms like Austin, Hillman, Singer and Standard made their own engines whilst those that did not speedily acquired a supplier. There were also numerous newcomers who copied pre-war US ideas by buying in components as cheaply as possible. A typical example was Clyno of Wolverhampton, which between 1922 and 1929, when it went bankrupt, made around 40,000 cars, many of which had Coventry Climax engines. Angus Sanderson tried a similar formula at a former armaments factory in County Durham. It used Tylor engines and collapsed after making a few thousand cars.

Bean did rather better but even it could not afford to produce a six-cylinder engine for its 1926-8 18/50 model as cheaply as its Black Country neighbour, Meadows. Henry Meadows had worked for Clyno and built up a proprietary-engine business with well over sixty customers in the 1920s. Contemporaries included Greenwood & Batley of Leeds, which made sleeve valve engines for Argyll; Hick Hargreaves of Bolton, with a 15.9 hp side-valve four in 1921 that found few customers; and British Anzani.

Alexandre Anzani was born in Milan in 1889 and made engines in France from 1906. His aero motors were made under licence in Britain from about 1910 but from 1919 motorcycle and car engines, notably for Morgan, predominated at British Anzani in London. AC ordered two thousand, and two of its directors joined the board of British Anzani. Some engines were also made in the factory of Cubitt, an AC associate. Stirling Moss's father Alfred raced an Anzani-powered Crouch at Brooklands in 1923.

*A Bayern Motor advertisement of 1920. The company, which became better known as BMW, was formed from various aero firms in 1917. It had about ten customers for truck engines and became a car-maker in 1928 when it purchased Dixi (then making versions of the Austin 7).*

9

# The British Anzani Engine Co., Ltd.

Telephone Nos.:
WILLESDEN 2770-2771.

Please reply to the Company, and refer to—

Your ref:

Our ref: **JWS/NY.**

*Works and Registered Offices*

British Anzani Works,

30, 31 & 32, Scrubbs Lane, Willesden,

LONDON, N.W. 10 _____ **12th July** _____ 192 **4**

*Part of a letter from British Anzani to a prospective customer in 1924. Because of financial difficulties the engine-builder diversified into horticultural tractors and outboard motors, followed by the unsuccessful Astra light car of 1956–9.*

E.T.W.Addyman Esq,
Engineer.
Starbeck.
  Harrogate,

Dear Sir,

   In reply to your letter to hand asking for details of an1100 c.c. air cooled engine suitable for racing and hill climbing, we have pleasure in handing you herewith a copy of our catalogue which gives details of our 9 HP V twin sports engine which is fitted with 8 overhead valves.

   This engine has put up some very excellent performances in the Morgan Three Wheeler, and would we think be suitable for your purpose provided you arrange it in the Chassis in such a way that it can be kept cool. In the Morgan, you will recollect, it is placed right in front of the machine.

   The engine has a bore and stroke of 85 X 95, 1075 c.c. and develops 28.6 HP at 3000, 34.5 at 3500 and 37 HP at 4000.

   The trade price of the engine is £40.0.0. An M.L. magneto with the firing points set at an angle of 57o with bevel driving wheels for same £4.10.0. and AMAC 2 lever or Zenith No.22 carburetter £1.16.0. These prices are nett c.o.d. our works.

   You will, of course, understand that this is a racing engine, and does not therefore come under our usual guarantee which applies to our standard engines, and if you think it will be suitable for your requirements we shall be delighted to send you a full sized blue print.

Gustav Maclure, who had worked at Anzani, designed an engine called the Plus-Power. It was used by Frazer Nash and up to fifty were also used in Horstman cars. In 1927, following difficulties not least with its AC contract, British Anzani was sold to Frazer Nash. One engine design was separately developed at British Anzani's former works and became the 1500 cc overhead camshaft 50 bhp four-cylinder British Vulpine. British Anzani soon left Frazer Nash and, with fresh backing, became best-known for outboard motors and Iron Horse horticultural tractors.

Meanwhile, Albert Gough, an engine-tuner at Frazer Nash, developed his own engine for his sports cars. These were produced by Beans Industries, the engineering firm and former car-maker, which was still making engines in the 1990s for Bedford and Reliant.

Granville Bradshaw's engines were best known in motorcycles and the Belsize and ABC light cars. Some had oil cooling, instead of water or air, and the majority were made by James Walmsley's Marathon Engineering Works in Preston.

Blackburne engines were also more often found in motorcycles. They were made in Surrey from 1908 by Burney & Blackburne, but it appears that some were produced by Gillet & Stevens of Bookham, notably the overhead camshaft six-cylinder 12/45 hp engine designed for Invicta by H. J. Hatch.

10

*A view of Lycoming's premises in 1927. No doubt the 'airplane' that produced the view was powered by Lycoming, a name which survived the collapse of E. L. Cord's car interests to become the aircraft firm AVCO-Lycoming in 1938.*

The Peters engine, of Belgian origin, was produced in Kingston upon Thames for cars such as Carrow, Mascotte, Castle Three and Junior Sports, all short-lived. This engine should not be confused with the well-known Petter from Yeovil, used mostly for farm and industrial purposes but tried also in the Seaton-Petter car and Shefflex lorry.

The biggest car-assemblers in the USA (where almost 2 million vehicles were made in 1919 and over 5 million in 1929) worked in tens of thousands of units, and for a time proprietary-engine makers kept pace. Continental supplied certain models of Paige-Detroit, Abbott-Detroit, Dodge, Columbia, Saxon, Thomas, Patterson, Moon, Davis, Jordan, Velie, Selden and Brisoe, and well over a hundred others. By 1932 its factory at Muskegon, Michigan, had made 3.5 million Continental Red Seal vehicle engines but was being increasingly threatened by the tendency for fewer, larger car-makers to produce their own major components. However, Continental was able to claim that 53 per cent of US truck-makers had used its engines, that it had three hundred agricultural and industrial clients and that it made more aero engines in its power band than all its rivals combined.

Another firm to move to aero engines after the Wall Street crash was Lycoming. By 1923 it had built 200,000 vehicle engines and had fifty commercial vehicle and almost as many car customers around the world. With users such as Auburn, Elcar, Gardner, McFarlan, Paige and Roamer cars, plus Atterbury, Gramm, IHC, Republic, Ruggles and Stewart trucks, output had reached almost half a million in 1927 when Lycoming was acquired by the Auburn–Cord–Duesenberg car empire. As well as the existing Auburns, it made engines for the famous coffin-nosed, front-wheel-drive L-29 Cord.

Duesenberg, the makers of the USA's most costly car, had also made engines for numerous other car firms since the Mason of 1906. In addition, it sold a design to Rochester Motors, which had several car customers up to 1924, including Argonne, Premocar and Kenworthy.

Cord had also acquired engine-maker Ansted in 1926. Frank B. Ansted had controlled the Lexington car factory for five years when in 1918 he bought the Teetor-Hartley engine business, which since 1910 had supplied Pilot, American Underslung, Empire and Auburn. Ansted supplied Lexington as well as one model of Durant (the B22) and the Australian Six. The Teetor brothers had entered the engine business when H. C. Stutz

11

could not get enough Continental engines for his American Underslungs.
Ferro Machine & Foundry of Cleveland, Ohio, made unusually small four-cylinder side-valve 1.4 litre engines for Saxon and overhead valve V eights for Briscoe, Scripps-Booth and Jackson in 1917–18. Henry Souther, the vice-president in 1914–16, went on to be an engineer at Locomobile, at Knox and at Columbia.
Northway of Detroit supplied Jackson, Sheridan, Cole, Auburn, Regal, Cartercar and Marathon. It made four, six and V eight units but disappeared into General Motors after being purchased by Olds(mobile) in 1917.
Le Roi from the Milwaukee Machine Tool Company had Sterling, Astra, Birch, Partin-Palmer and Seneca amongst its customers from 1916 to 1923. The 1916 Brown car used a Le Roi with an Allis-Chalmers electric starter. Le Roi then became better known for industrial, horticultural and farm engines before reappearing with a range of Roiline truck engines as part of Waukesha in the 1960s.
Carrico Motor Company of Cincinnati made air-cooled, horizontally opposed twins for several US high-wheelers around 1910 and also made a four-cylinder air-cooled engine for the Wolfe car.
Golden, Belknap & Schwartz used their initials from 1910 to 1924 on a range of engines used by several obscure makers. Beaver of Milwaukee lasted into the 1920s too, having had Luverne and Meteor amongst an extensive but not very successful list of car-makers stretching back to 1903.
Midwest grew out of the Atlas Motor Car Company, which had supplied engines to Hudson in 1909–10. It acquired a Knight sleeve valve licence and, as Lyons Atlas, from 1912 became an important supplier of engines to such firms as HCS and Handley-Knight. Its factory in Indianapolis covered 30 acres (12 hectares) by 1927 but it was in serious financial trouble. Silent sleeve valves were used successfully in place of poppet valves in makes such as Panhard, Daimler and Willys for twenty years from 1910. R. & V. Engineering made them for Moline-Knight and others.

In France Ruby engines, usually with overhead valves, were widely used by dozens of light car firms after Godefroy & Lévêque started making them in 1909. There were so few customers left by 1935 that Ruby acquired the Georges Irat car firm and managed to sell 1500 of these front-wheel-driven cars with 1100 cc Ruby engines in the years up to the Second World War. Afterwards Georges

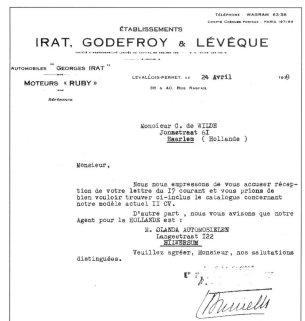

*A 1939 letter from the combined makers of Ruby engines and Georges Irat cars. Ruby had made its own cars from 1910 until the early 1920s, when it abandoned them to concentrate on engines for others.*

Right: *Rivals CD and CIME share a page in a 1925 catalogue for engine-buyers. CIME had over twenty-five customers and specialised in small overhead valve motors before adding a 1.7 litre inclined-valve six in 1927.*

Below: *JAP stood for John Albert Prestwich, born in London in 1874. Starting in 1902, JAP had made some 50,000 engines by 1914, mostly for motorcycles but also for light cars like this Morgan. It supplied many more cars in the 1920s and in the 1950s built numerous engines for the 500 cc racing-car formula. The firm eventually merged with its rival Villiers and its Tottenham works, employing 2500 in its heyday, closed in 1963.*

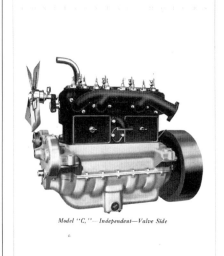

Model "C," — Independent—Valve Side

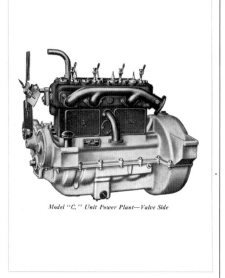

Model "C," Unit Power Plant—Valve Side

## THE CONTINENTAL CERTAINTIES:
SILENCE - POWER - ENDURANCE - SPEED - ECONOMY - FLEXIBILITY

*The Continental Model C available in 3.7 or 4.6 litre sizes. In 1920 only 29 out of 186 makers of US trucks made their own engines. Continental supplied the greatest number of the others (76) followed by Buda (33), Wisconsin (10) and Waukesha (9). Eleven other engine-makers catered for the remainder.*

Irat made his own DOG diesels for tractors and trucks.

SCAP had a slightly wider range of engines than its rivals, from the typical 850 cc up to 3 litres, and supplied the well-known BNC sports cars. As the Société des Constructions Automobiles Parisiennes it built cars from 1914 to 1929, the last of which was a 2 litre straight eight.

Charles Chapuis and Charles Dornier established Chapuis Dornier or CD at Besançon in 1905. They made single-cylinder engines, followed by a four in 1909 with a patented cylinder head incorporating exhaust and inlet manifolds in the casting. In 1910 a move to Puteaux to be near the Paris-based motor industry was followed by massive expansion using designs from the Swiss engineer Sigmund Gerster. These incorporated side-exhaust and overhead inlet valves (like 1930s Coventry Climax and later Rolls-Royce and Rover). Over two thousand were sold in 1910. British customers included Waverley, Gamage, Jackson, Pilot and Hampton (plus the 14.3 and 20 hp post-war Storey) and it eventually counted amongst its nearly a hundred customers worldwide the French sporting car-makers Benjamin, Derby, Rally and Senechal. Much of this trade was lost to its rival SCAP, which produced an improved 1100 cc engine that from 1926 could be supercharged. (Meadows devotees Lea Francis tried one boosted by Cozette.) CD's typically small customers all succumbed to the Great Depression and CD itself closed in 1935.

Buchet was founded in Levallois-Perret in 1888 to make arc lights. After about ten years it began making engines and applying overhead valve conversions to de Dion-Bouton motors. Having made a V eight aero engine in 1906, Buchet started building cars in 1910. It also built engines for others and by the time it expired around 1930 it

14

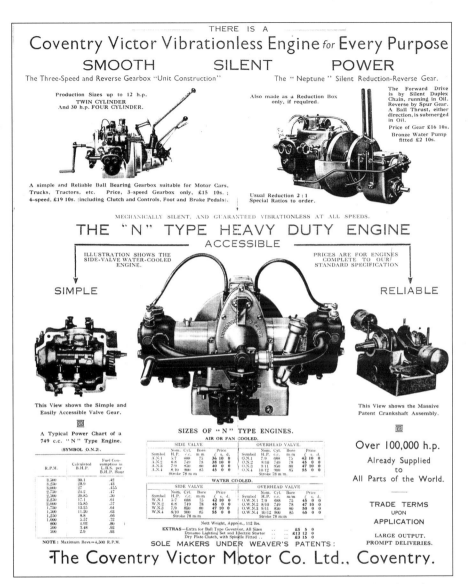

*From 1911 Coventry Victor made horizontally opposed, twin-cylinder engines (resembling those of Jowett, another firm willing to supply outsiders). This illustration shows details of the 1920s range. The firm also built its own cars and vans up to 1939.*

had counted twenty-three car-makers in France, Britain, Austria and Belgium amongst its clients.

Fondu was a Belgian car-maker from 1906 to 1912, after which it supplied engines to others. T. B. André was its British agent from 1910 right through to the 1930s. Engine production was quoted as fifty per month in 1912 and Turner of

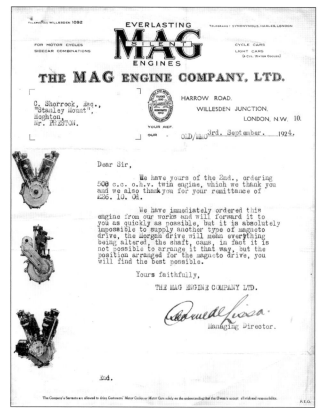

*A letter to Chris Shorrock of supercharger fame from MAG, a Swiss firm with British links that also made Motosacoche motorcycles and Maximag cars. The reverse of the letter showed air-cooled singles and twins of 250–1000 cc and four-cylinder 1100 cc water-cooled car engines (see below).*

Wolverhampton was a customer.

Just as BMW motorcycle engines were used in German light cars, so the Swiss MAG was found in a number of cars made in various countries, Train engines powered several diminutive French cars, and JAP, Villiers, Precision and Blackburne served the British market. US Henderson and Harley Davidson motorcycle engines were also found in cars. Engines named Precision were the work of the designer F. A. Baker, who had gained US experience in Cleveland and sold his British firm to Beardmore.

*MAG engines of c.1924. (From left to right) Overhead valve engine, racing type, 500–1000 cc; four cylinder 1100 cc light car engine; overhead valve engine, racing type, 250–350 cc.*

This is a CLM opposed-piston, single-cylinder, two-stroke diesel undergoing tests in England in 1930. A Le Zebre displayed at the 1931 Paris Salon was similarly powered and was probably the world's first diesel car to be offered for sale.

# The other principal makers

Founded in 1870, Dorman of Stafford claimed to have been making engines 'before the Red Flag Act was abolished' (1896). Numerous car and commercial-vehicle clients are listed in its later sales ledgers, including Little Greg, Westcar, Eric Longden, Tiny, Maltby, Santler, Vulcan, Surrey, Palladium, Caledon, Autocrat, Merryweather and Airedale. Output of a thousand engines per month was claimed in 1920 but this dwindled as smaller makers foundered, and after the mid 1920s most of its engines went to the commercial-vehicle makers Karrier, Garner, Pagefield, Lacre and W. & G. du Cros. Dorman's plight had been worsened by the departure of the sales director John Dorman and then in 1921 the designer R. S. Crump to the new Meadows engine business.

Dorman, however, was more successful with commercial vehicles and added a twin-cylinder 35 bhp diesel to its range of 8.5–100 bhp petrol engines in 1930. From the 1940s it concentrated on industrial engines before a final fling with a road-going 235 bhp V eight in 1970. It was bought by English Electric in 1961 and, having passed through GEC, it was finally acquired by Perkins for $30 million in 1994.

*A 1920 Dorman 1490 cc side-valve engine. The fact that the RAC horsepower rating calculated for taxation purposes matched its brake horsepower at 1000 rpm was largely coincidental and it could develop increased power at a more usable 1500 rpm.*

*Dorman managed to replace dwindling car customers with commercial-vehicle firms, particularly with its diesels of 1930 onwards. Here a Dorman-Ricardo-powered Guy delivers engines for export.*

Coventry Simplex and Coventry Climax were both formed by H. Pelham Lee, who had worked for Daimler in Coventry. With a Danish partner he built half a dozen Lee Stroyer cars in 1903 and then started Coventry Simplex in part of a former Humber factory in Paynes Lane, Coventry. Alexander Craig of Maudslay (and later a Rover director) did the initial designs with help from Alan Lea of Lea-Francis. A thousand engines were supplied to GWK between 1911 and 1915 with others to firms such as Turner and Foy Steele in a range from 8 to 40 hp. Following disagreements, H. Pelham Lee sold the business and in 1917 acquired the Johnson Smith Engine Company, then making generator sets, to create Coventry Climax.

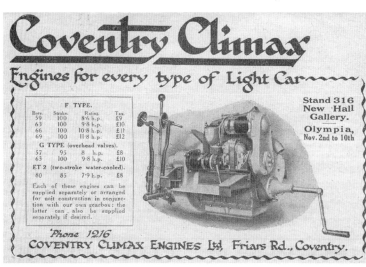

*A 1923 advertisement showing part of the range of Coventry Climax Engines Ltd. It was still competing with Coventry Simplex, from which it had separated in 1917.*

Coventry Climax gradually eclipsed Coventry Simplex (itself making fifty engines per week in March 1920, notably for GWK, Lea-Francis, Eric-Campbell and Ashton-Evans cars). Early Coventry Climax customers included Albatros, Marseal, Horstman, Bayliss-Thomas, Clyno (briefly selling four hundred per week in 1926) and Swift. Lee's son Leonard worked for Arthur Grice, the G of GWK, making his Unit cars, some with Bovier engines, before joining Coventry Climax. Following the Wall Street crash Lee, then employing around a hundred men, watched newspaper hoardings in the streets of Coventry as one by one his customers declared bankruptcy. In 1930 an inlet over exhaust valve engine was designed and Coventry Climax gradually regained some car customers, for example Marendaz Special, Crossley, Morgan, AJS and Triumph. They also made copies of Lycoming engines for Gilford coaches, did subcontract work on the V eight Standard and created engines for the first Harry Ferguson tractors. By the mid 1930s 90,000 Coventry Climax engines had been sold. As Britain re-armed, engines originally intended for use in Swifts were fitted on portable fire pumps (of which 25,000 had been built by the end of the Second World War). Forklift trucks, racing-car engines and pumps kept Coventry Climax in business after the war, and the firm joined Jaguar in 1963 (as did Meadows in the following year). A notable road car powered by Coventry Climax was the Lotus Elite, new in 1959.

Henry Meadows, a machining expert, left Clyno to build his first Meadows gearbox in 1920 (for Vulcan). He followed this in 1922 with engines, which were supplied in

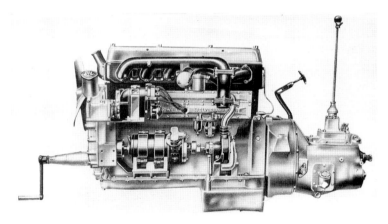

*Meadows became famous for its six-cylinder engines from the mid 1920s. This is a 77 bhp at 2000 rpm 5528 cc 6EW model from about 1930, intended for 'buses and high speed road transport of deluxe character'. The late 1920s range included sixes of 3301–7983 cc and fours of 918–3686 cc.*

substantial numbers, often more profitably with gearboxes, to British Ensign, Salmons, Phoenix, Hampton and Seabrook, and from 1923 to Autocrat, Airedale and Lea-Francis (which, with over four thousand engines, became the most important vintage customer). As shoestring light-car makers collapsed, healthier ones like Lagonda, Invicta and Frazer Nash remained, requiring larger, more sophisticated and consequently more expensive engines. Meadows also had a captive market for commercial-vehicle engines from its near neighbours in Wolverhampton, AJS and Guy.

*A page from Meadows's order book for its engines with gearboxes from 1923, showing numerous car firms including Lea-Francis, which became its biggest customer. All the engines are of 1247 cc capacity apart from 1496 cc units used by Seabrook and by Kennedy (who made the Rob Roy in Glasgow).*

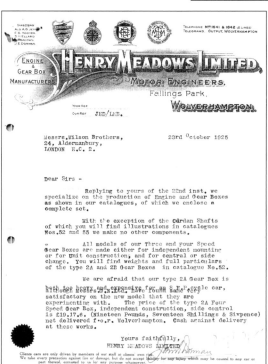

*Henry Meadows was joined by John Dorman, a member of the family behind Dorman engines, here writing to Wilson Brothers, a firm that toyed with plans to produce cars in quantity but actually made very few.*

Buda engines gained their unusual name from a town in Illinois where George Chalender established his railway equipment factory in 1881. He moved to a 6 acre (2.4 hectare) factory at Harvey, Chicago, and added engines to his product range in 1910. Over the years Buda had 106 truck customers but only ten who made cars (including Biddle and Lambert). Buda made engines for the Jeffrey Quad, an advanced First World War US Army truck, and in 1924 introduced a six-cylinder coach engine and claimed to have 32 per cent of the US heavy-vehicle market. In 1926 it acquired rights to the diesel made by MAN, the company where Dr Rudolf Diesel did his pioneering experiments. Although the early Buda-MAN was for industrial and marine purposes, by 1935 Buda was offering vehicle diesels. In 1953 Buda was bought by Allis-Chalmers, itself a maker of farm machinery and engines, which subsequently offered truck engines under its own name.

Hercules of Canton, Ohio, was operating from about 1910 and ultimately became a division of the Hupp Corporation, which had built Hupmobile cars from 1909 to 1940. In the mid 1930s Hercules claimed to be 'the world's largest maker of diesels for road transport'. From 1949 Hercules had links with Hispano-Suiza-Bugatti and made the French firm's diesels in the USA. H. H. Timken, Junior, of the eponymous bearings firm, was a director in the 1950s, and in 1966 Hercules, by then incorporating Hall Scott, disappeared into the White group. Having made a 106 bhp six for White trucks,

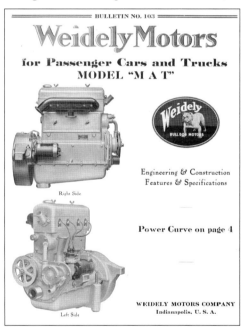

Above left: *Hercules supplied Federal and Diamond T, whose US trucks were well known in Europe. This advertisement dates from 1935, when an additional factory was opened near Continental at Muskegon, Michigan.*

Above right: *Walter Weidely was founder and chief engineer of the car-maker Premier in 1903. His Weidely Motors supplied Chalmers, HAL, Owen, Kissel, HCS, Auburn and others from 1913. A few even bought his 1916 6.4 litre V twelves. Weidely Motors collapsed after Stutz cancelled its engine contract in 1924. This is from a late catalogue for push-rod overhead valve motors developing up to 40 bhp.*

21

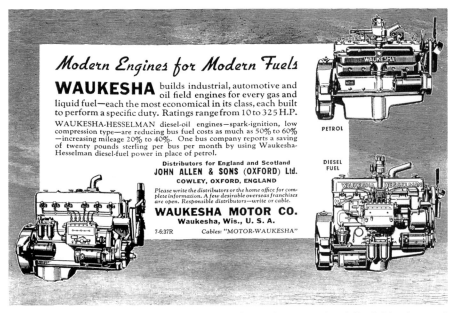

A 1937 advertisement for Waukesha petrol, semi-diesel (Hesselman patent) and diesel (Ricardo patent) engines. The British agents were best known for their Allen motor scythes but also operated heavy plant and made cranes.

it became independent once more in the 1970s.

Between 1904 and 1907 Herschell-Spillman made cars in North Tonawanda, New York, before supplying engines to dozens of other firms, from Berkshire and Roamer to Dixie Flyer and Dupont.

Wisconsin operated in Milwaukee from 1910 to 1928, making thousands of engines for First World War trucks. It also supplied numerous cars, amongst which in the 1920s were Wasp, Jacquet, HCS, Dupont and McFarlan, the last two with large and refined six-cylinder units. In 1954 it claimed to be the largest maker of 3–36 horsepower air-cooled engines.

Waukesha, from the town of that name in Wisconsin, began in 1906, early car users being the 40 hp Fawick and 20 hp Wright. The First World War boosted truck-engine output (notably for the standardised Liberty) and Waukesha came to specialise in this area. Around 1930 it was reckoned to charge 25–30 per cent more than its rivals but, as with Gardner diesels in Britain, long life and minimal downtime were assured and sales of eight thousand engines per month were quoted in 1929. The Swedish Hesselman spark-ignition, low-compression 20–300 bhp semi-diesel was adopted in the 1930s and in 1935 Waukesha also built 100–140 bhp Comet full diesels licensed by Ricardo plus 12–200 bhp petrol engines. It was still making big petrol engines for road haulage in the 1960s as well as naturally aspirated and turbo diesels including V twelves up to 384 bhp. It also controlled Le Roi and became a division of Dresser Industries, which made the giant Haulpak dump-trucks.

*Gardners were shoehorned into several cars. A 4LW-powered Bentley was the highest-placed British entry in the 1933 Monte Carlo Rally. Here a Wolseley is fitted with the even lighter 4LK using magnesium alloy. One in a Lagonda averaged over 40 mpg during a hard drive through North Wales and a member of the Gardner family used a 6LK-engined Invicta to travel at up to 100 mph.*

# Changing times: 1930–2000

The big diesel success was Gardner. Its refined and economical industrial and marine engines built in Manchester were discovered by bus operators in 1930 (by when over 29,000 engines had been sold) and soon dominated the British, French and Belgian market for large-capacity proprietary diesels. Only the largest lorry and bus manufacturers like AEC, Berliet, Mercedes-Benz, MAN and Leyland were able to develop their own successful diesels in-house. Saurer in Switzerland also managed to

*McLaren was renowned for steam engineering, but it acquired British manufacturing rights to Benz diesels. The first diesel lorry to run in Britain was a Mercedes-Benz in 1928; this advertisement dates from 1931.*

23

*Frank Perkins (1889–1967) (far left), who from 1932 made the first diesels that were sufficiently light and fast-revving to be interchangeable with petrol engines. The modest first premises are shown (near left). Output of a few dozen engines had grown to a thousand per year in 1939.*

license its designs around the world. Gardner supplied many chassis at the expensive high-quality end of the market – including Foden, ERF, Atkinson, Bernard, Latil, Corbitt and Miesse – and eventually passed to Perkins in 1986.

Cheaper and lighter diesels were developed by Frank Perkins in Peterborough. His family made Barford & Perkins motor rollers and with fellow engineer Charles Chapman he produced the world's first high-speed diesel (compatible with petrol-engine gearboxes and rear-axle ratios) at Peterborough in 1932. This was the Vixen

*Perkins's new Peterborough factory, opened in 1947, had grown substantially by 1980, when around 9 million Perkins diesels had been sold.*

24

and it was joined by the Fox and the Wolf, the last breaking six world speed records when installed in a racing car in 1935. Chapman designed their first six in 1936, the famous P6, which was produced for some twenty years. By 1939 Perkins was selling a thousand diesels a year and in 1947 the company opened what is still claimed to be the largest factory in the world exclusively producing diesel engines.

Perkins was bought by Massey Ferguson in 1959 and three years later Frank Perkins retired. The firm's first V eight was offered in 1965 and Perkins was making half a million engines per year by 1975. An attempt to dieselise the Rover V eight was made in 1982 but more successful was the Prima, used in other Leyland group cars and vans. The firm subsequently joined Caterpillar, the maker of earth-moving machinery, whose diesels became popular proprietary units from the 1950s.

Morgan typified the plight of the car-assemblers when decimated sales compelled it to turn to a rival in 1934. Ford's engines were cheaper and better than most proprietary units and many specialist cars used them from the 1930s to the 1960s. They also spawned the sporting Cosworth engines. In addition to small British Ford engines, big US Fords were found in such late 1930s Anglo-American hybrids as Allard, Jensen and Atalanta. Jensen also used Nash engines, whilst Lammas favoured Graham, and Railton sold over a thousand with Hudson Terraplane components. The most successful of these hybrids in the 1930s became SS Jaguar, using engines from Standard (also favoured by Morgan and small Railtons). At the end of the 1930s Standard bought Triumph, a car-maker that depended latterly, like Crossley and the first Morgan four-wheelers, on Coventry Climax.

In the USA as in Britain commercial-vehicle operators continued to buy a significant number of vehicles from the smaller custom-builders. Clessie L. Cummins had made the Monitor car at Columbus, Ohio, from 1915 using GB & S or Continental engines. He obtained rights to the Dutch Hvid farm and marine engine and soon abandoned cars to experiment with diesels. In 1929 he perfected a camshaft-activated individual injector system for each cylinder, which became a Cummins hallmark. Cummins

*This was virtually the whole of the Cummins workforce of 1931 with a Cummins diesel-powered Duesenberg racing car. Although not the fastest at Indianapolis, it was the first to manage the entire 500 miles (805 km) without refuelling.*

installed his diesel in a Packard at the end of 1929 and drove it 800 miles (about 1300 km) to the New York Automobile Show. After that he often used cars and even racing cars to demonstrate the speed and frugality of his engines, but it was the heavy-truck market that Cummins came to dominate. Auburn used S c h w i t z e r - C u m m i n s superchargers on some of its cars and in 1935 there were serious plans to market Auburn diesel airport limousines but these foundered with the collapse of the Auburn–Cord–Duesenberg empire. Cummins's first profits did not come until 1937, at which time the firm had a workforce of two hundred. By 1970 it employed 14,000,

Above left: *Apart from suppliers of microcar engines like Kubota and Lombardini, one of the few remaining makers of proprietary car engines in the 1990s was VM (standing for 1947 founders Vancini and Martelli), which from the 1980s supplied Alfa Romeo, Rover and Chrysler amongst others. Two sister companies were Isotta Fraschini, which made cars between 1900 and 1947, and whose ID36 turbo-charged V six is shown, and Ducati, which joined the group in 1980 and made motorcycles and diesels up to 25 bhp.*

Above right: *Leonard P. Lee (left) of Coventry Climax shows off his 1.5 litre V eight FWMV engine developing over 200 bhp to the racing driver Jim Clark and the creator of Lotus, Colin Chapman.*

Above: *When the capacity of Formula One racing engines leapt from 1.5 to 3 litres in 1966 Mike Costin and Keith Duckworth unveiled their Cosworth DFV (double four-valve) engine financed by Ford. With Jim Clark in a Lotus 49, this won its first race and went on to more than 150 Grand Prix victories. Here Tom Wheatcroft of Donington tries the Cosworth four-wheel-drive Grand Prix car of 1969.*

Right: *The Detroit two-stroke diesel powered tanks, trucks and this Allis-Chalmers crawler in the Second World War. The Cleveland plant, which made industrial diesels, had originated with the Winton cars of 1898–1924. Winton also made proprietary engines from 1912 and this business was bought by General Motors in 1930.*

## PREVIEW OF TOMORROW'S POWER

IF you want a glimpse of how to-morrow's hard jobs will be done, look at what is doing the tough war jobs today — such jobs as building airfields in the jungle.

Look in tanks and trucks, in land-ing barges and patrol vessels, in tractors and auxiliaries. You'll find General Motors Diesel Engines pack-ing them with power.

This grueling service is emphasiz-ing the virtues of GM Diesels—high-lighting their ruggedness—showing

how little fuel they use, and low-cost fuel at that.

With the war won, our expanded facilities will be turned to peacetime needs, and these engines will be avail-able for many applications where America will need dependable, eco-nomical power.

*Even before the war, truckers knew the economies of GM Diesels. When peace comes, the expanded manufacture born of war will make this motive power more widely available than ever before.*

**BACK THE ATTACK—WITH WAR BONDS**

GENERAL MOTORS
**DIESEL POWER**

ENGINES.....15 to 250 H.P.....DETROIT DIESEL ENGINE DIVISION, Detroit, Mich.

ENGINES...150 to 2000 H.P...CLEVELAND DIESEL ENGINE DIVISION, Cleveland, Ohio

LOCOMOTIVES...................ELECTRO-MOTIVE DIVISION, La Grange, Ill.

27

having opened its first overseas factory (in 1957) in Scotland, and was supplying most specialist truck firms in Britain and the USA.

Apart from Caterpillar, Cummins's main rival was Detroit, which had been established in 1937 by General Motors to make two-stroke diesels. The 1.5 millionth was produced in 1972, and in 1988 the business was sold to the Penske Corporation, which at the time also owned VM of Italy. The joint business subsequently became part of Daimler Chrysler. In 2001 VM had a thousand employees making forty thousand engines *per annum*, with the Chrysler Voyager, the Jeep and some mid-sized Hyundai models amongst its users.

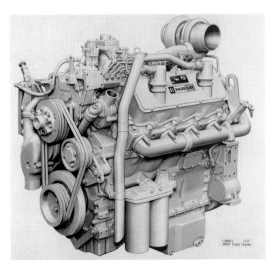

*A 1977 Caterpillar 18 litre V eight diesel developing up to 450 bhp with turbocharger and aftercooler. Most US heavy trucks have offered Caterpillar, Cummins and Detroit options since the 1950s.*

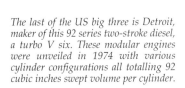

*The last of the US big three is Detroit, maker of this 92 series two-stroke diesel, a turbo V six. These modular engines were unveiled in 1974 with various cylinder configurations all totalling 92 cubic inches swept volume per cylinder.*

28

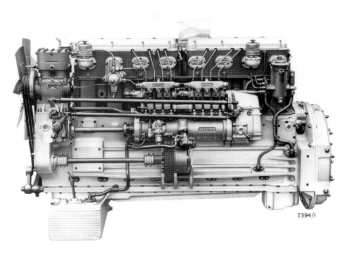

*A Gardner 8LXB of 1979, one of the most aesthetically pleasing, efficient and longest-lasting non-turbo diesels ever built. Straight eight was a most unusual configuration and unlike rival V eights it would not fit under the average truck cab. This and its high cost limited sales, as did its relatively low power output of 250 bhp from 14 litres. The fact that it had an almost flat torque curve from 1000 to 1850 maximum rpm gave it amazing lugging ability.*

Caterpillar established sales and marketing links with Daimler Chrysler in 2000, having previously taken over Perkins, which had itself acquired most remaining British proprietary-engine makers, including Rolls-Royce diesels in 1983. The latter was an offshoot of the famous aero-engine and car firm that had moved into the Sentinel commercial-vehicle factory in Shrewsbury in the mid 1950s, where it developed its renowned Eagle road-vehicle diesels, which ultimately powered 40 per cent of vehicles over 28 tons in Britain.

In 2001 proprietary engines were present in only a few Italian- and Japanese-powered microcars, with most specialist car-makers (mainly sports cars in Britain)

*The origins of Deutz are linked with four-stroke pioneer N. A. Otto (1832–91). Gottlieb Daimler and Wilhelm Maybach worked at Deutz before making automobiles. Deutz has made engines ever since, its most familiar being air-cooled diesels developed in the 1940s and used in Magirus-Deutz and many other vehicles. This example dates from the 1950s.*

*Frisky* **Family Three** Four Seater

★ ELEGANT
★ ECONOMICAL
★ ROOMY
★ RELIABLE

Styled by the famous
Italian designer
GIOVANNI MICHELOTTI

FRISKY

FRISKY CARS (1959) LIMITED · PARK LANE · WOLVERHAMPTON · ENGLAND

*The post-Suez fuel crisis of the 1950s resulted in a revival of interest in microcars. Meadows's answer to the German bubble-cars was the Frisky. This 1960 example has an Excelsior 246 cc two-cylinder two-stroke, developing 10.75 bhp at 5000 rpm. British Anzani also experimented with microcars without success.*

Right: *Large petrol engines could still exist alongside diesels because of the low fuel prices in the USA when Waukesha produced this advertisement in 1959. It shows a Peterbilt truck with an engine that could rarely have exceeded 3 mpg. Rival Continental offered a 240 bhp V eight petrol engine in the late 1950s.*

Below: *The CLM opposed-piston two-stroke was gradually ousted by more conventional diesels in the 1950s. Peugeot, having experimented with a diesel car in the 1920s, acquired CLM. These initials were eventually replaced on Peugeot diesels by the name Indenor. This 1972 XLD developed 45 bhp at 5000 rpm from a mere 1255 cc. Note the strange angle of the belt to run the fan at the front of a transverse installation.*

*On the milk run*

**...OR ANY RUN**

PETERBILT truck—tire size: 10.00 x 20; rear axle ratio: 5.91; gross vehicle weight: 76,800 lbs.—is powered with Waukesha 145-GZB engine.

**where the pay-off
is on pay-load**

**WAUKESHA**
*transport*
**ENGINES**

Waukesha 143-GZB High Output Engine, 5⅛-in. bore x 6-in. stroke, 817 cu. in. displacement, up to 260 hp at 2400 rpm.

WAUKESHA MOTOR COMPANY
WAUKESHA, WISCONSIN

New York • Tulsa • Los Angeles

Factories: Waukesha, Wisconsin and Clinton, Iowa

Short runs or long hauls—the pay-off is on pay-load that gets there faster. A rare combination of extra power plus extra speed, with rugged reliability—the Waukesha 145-GZB High Output Engine keeps trucks on schedule with day-after-day all-ways-dependable regularity. It's a high compression, overhead valve gasoline engine with interchangeable cylinder heads, removable wet sleeve cylinders, water-heated intake manifold, vibration dampener, heavy-duty aluminum pistons, 7-bearing, 3½-inch crankshaft fully counterbalanced and many other fully-proved features, all detailed in Bulletin 1553.

*Uniquely, since its first cars in 1910 Morgan has never made its own engines. Proprietary types have included Anzani, JAP, Blackburne and Coventry Climax, whilst engines from other car-makers have included Ford, Standard, Rover and, for the all-aluminium Aero 8 of 2000 shown here, a BMW 4.4 litre V eight developing 286 bhp to provide a top speed of 160 mph.*

having to buy engines from rivals like Rover, Ford and BMW (which had itself started out as a maker of proprietary engines). Only amongst the heavy-commercial-vehicle makers owned or inspired by US companies is the future of proprietary engines still relatively secure.

*The Ford 2.5 litre Duratec-engined Noble M12 GTO entered production in 2001. Its V six developed 310 bhp and one hundred orders were taken at its first public showing.*

# Further reading

Clew, Jeff. *JAP: the End of an Era.* Haynes, 1988.
Clew, Jeff. *JAP: the Vintage Years.* Haynes, 1988.
Cruikshank, Jeffrey, and Sicilia, David. *The Engine That Could.* Harvard Business School Press, 1997. (A history of Cummins.)
Georgano, Nick. *The Beaulieu Encyclopaedia of the Automobile* (two volumes). The Stationery Office, 2000.
Hassan, Walter, and Robson, Graham. *Climax in Coventry.* Motor Racing Publications, 1975.
Knight, Patrick. *A–Z of British Stationary Engines.* Kelsey Publishing, 1996.
Moon, John F. *Rudolf Diesel and the Diesel Engine.* Priory Press, 1974.

Other sources include books on one-make car histories and magazines such as *The Autocar* and *The Motor* and the plethora of rivals that were published in veteran and vintage times. The principal magazines to touch on the history of proprietary engines in modern times are *The Automobile* (Holmerise, Seven Hills Road, Cobham, Surrey KT11 1ES) and *Stationary Engine Magazine* (Berrys Hill, Cudham, Kent TN16 3AG).

# Places to visit

Classic and vintage rallies abound with vehicles powered by proprietary engines, but it is often difficult to spot them as manufacturers often concealed their use of other firms' engines or even cheated by putting their own name on the engine. Vehicle owners and sometimes the event programme may be able to help.

Many of Dorman's records are housed at the County Records Office, Stafford, and the sales records of Meadows are held by the author, c/o Shire Publications. Many motor museums have proprietary engines on display either in or out of vehicles.

*Automobilia, Cornwall's Motor Museum,* The Old Mill, St Stephen, St Austell, Cornwall PL26 7RX. Telephone: 01726 823092. Website: www.3mc.co.uk/automobilia (Fifteen proprietary engines on display.)
*British Commercial Vehicle Museum,* King Street, Leyland, Preston, Lancashire PR5 1LE. Telephone: 01772 451011.
*Donington Grand Prix Collection,* Donington Park, Castle Donington, Derby DE74 2RP. Telephone: 01332 811027. Website: www.doningtoncollection.com
*East Anglia Transport Museum,* Chapel Road, Carlton Colville, Lowestoft, Suffolk NR33 8BL. Telephone 01502 518459. Website: www.eatm.org.uk
*Heritage Motor Centre,* British Motor Industry Heritage Trust, Gaydon, Warwick CV35 0BJ. Telephone: 01926 641188. Website: www.heritage.org.uk
*Museum of British Road Transport,* St Agnes Lane, Hales Street, Coventry CV1 1PN. Telephone: 024 76 832425. Website: www.mbrt.co.uk
*Museum of Transport – Manchester,* Boyle Street, Cheetham, Manchester M8 8UL. Telephone: 0161 205 2122. Website: www.gmts.co.uk
*National Motor Museum,* Beaulieu, Brockenhurst, Hampshire SO42 7ZN. Telephone: 01590 612345. Website: www.beaulieu.co.uk